LOVE
BY KATE CORTESI

DRAMATISTS
PLAY SERVICE
INC.

LOVE
Copyright © 2023, Kate Cortesi

All Rights Reserved

LOVE is fully protected under the copyright laws of the United States of America, and of all countries covered by the International Copyright Union (including the Dominion of Canada and the rest of the British Commonwealth), and of all countries covered by the Pan-American Copyright Convention, the Universal Copyright Convention, the Berne Convention, and of all countries with which the United States has reciprocal copyright relations. No part of this publication may be reproduced in any form by any means (electronic, mechanical, photocopying, recording, or otherwise), or stored in any retrieval system in any way (electronic or mechanical) without written permission of the publisher.

The English language stock and amateur stage performance rights in the United States, its territories, possessions and Canada for LOVE are controlled exclusively by Dramatists Play Service, 440 Park Avenue South, New York, NY 10016. **No professional or nonprofessional performance of the Play may be given without obtaining in advance the written permission of Dramatists Play Service and paying the requisite fee.**

All other rights, including without limitation motion picture, recitation, lecturing, public reading, radio broadcasting, television, video or sound recording, and the rights of translation into foreign languages are strictly reserved.

Inquiries concerning all other rights should be addressed to Creative Artists Agency, 405 Lexington Avenue, 19th Floor, New York, NY 10174. Attn: Alex Gold.

NOTE ON BILLING

Anyone receiving permission to produce LOVE is required to give credit to the Author as sole and exclusive Author of the Play on the title page of all programs distributed in connection with performances of the Play and in all instances in which the title of the Play appears, including printed or digital materials for advertising, publicizing or otherwise exploiting the Play and/or a production thereof. Please see your production license for font size and typeface requirements.

Be advised that there may be additional credits required in all programs and promotional material. Such language will be listed under the "Additional Billing" section of production licenses. It is the licensee's responsibility to ensure any and all required billing is included in the requisite places, per the terms of the license.

SPECIAL NOTE ON SONGS/RECORDINGS

Dramatists Play Service neither holds the rights to nor grants permission to use any songs or recordings mentioned in the Play. Permission for performances of copyrighted songs, arrangements or recordings mentioned in this Play is not included in our license agreement. The permission of the copyright owner(s) must be obtained for any such use. For any songs and/or recordings mentioned in the Play, other songs, arrangements, or recordings may be substituted provided permission from the copyright owner(s) of such songs, arrangements or recordings is obtained; or songs, arrangements or recordings in the public domain may be substituted.

NOTE ON EXCERPT

Parallel Lives: Five Victorian Marriages by Phyllis Rose
drawings by David Schorr
Copyright © 1982, Phyllis Rose
Published by Penguin Random House
Used with permission
All Rights Reserved

For our mothers.

LOVE was originally produced by Marin Theatre Company (Jasson Minadakis, Artistic Director; Keri Kellerman, Managing Director), Mill Valley, California. It opened on March 10, 2020. It was directed by Mike Donahue, the scenic design was by Stephanie Osin Cohen, the costume design was by Katie Nowacki, the lighting design was by Scott Zielinski, the sound design was by Madeleine Oldham, the projection design was by Teddy Hulsker, and the production stage manager was Liz Matos. The cast was as follows:

PENELOPE	Clea Alsip
OTIS	R. Ward Duffy
JAMIE	Bobak Cyrus Bakhtiari
VANESSA ("VEE")	Rebecca Schweitzer
WHITNEY/REBECCA	Mari Vial-Golden
RON/KEN	Robert Sicular

LOVE was developed by New Dramatists and at the Ojai Playwrights Conference (Robert Egan, Artistic Director/Producer) in August 2019.

CHARACTERS

PENELOPE
a woman in her late thirties in 2018, self-possessed

OTIS
a man in his late fifties in 2018, charming

JAMIE
a man in his late thirties in 2018, chill

VANESSA ("VEE")
a woman in her late thirties in 2018, sober

WHITNEY
a woman in her mid-thirties in 2018, starting over

REBECCA
a woman in her late thirties in 2004, aloof
(double cast with Whitney)

RON
a man in his fifties in 2018, strategic

KEN
a man in his fifties in 2004, protective
(double cast with Ron)

TIME

2018, 2009, 2004, and 2003

PLACE

Offices, cafés, bars, and bedrooms around New York City

NOTES FROM THE PLAYWRIGHT

Time
This is not a memory play. While the story does bounce around in time, the scenes in 2003, 2004, and 2009 must not be influenced by what the characters know in 2018. The audience will draw connections, of course, but as far as the people onstage are concerned, every scene takes place in the present. Allow 2003 and 2004 to brim with the wildness and naiveté of youth.

As you move from scene to scene, be clear about what year it is. There's no shame in projecting the year for the duration of the scene. With all the ambiguity in this play, I'm not interested in "what year is it?" ambiguity.

Otis
The character of Otis must never seem creepy or predatory. We should never witness anything close to sexual coercion. This man is buoyant, magnetic, and remarkably comfortable with himself. Think Peter Pan, not Bluebeard.

Love centers a New York City office that services poor and working-class families. The cast can and should be a diverse, authentic reflection of people from the city and those who migrate there for ambition and adventure. There is room here for all kinds of multicultural combinations in the cast. The one that must *never* happen, however, is a cast where Otis is a man of color while the rest of the cast is white; nor should Otis be a man of color while Penelope, Whitney, and Vanessa are all white.

Otis can be played by an actor of any race or ethnicity but he should palpably feel like someone who grew up running around the sidewalks of New York. There's a city kid hustle to him. And while his success as a small business founder and then figure in City Hall isn't exactly unlikely, it is certainly a point of pride in the community he grew up in.

The Set
I imagine the set as an origami-like folding-unfolding-refolding contraption. Can the set become a kind of kinetic sculpture during scene transitions? A café, a bar, an office, a bedroom—younger days, more mature days—can they all appear as different sides of the same shape? All boundaries are porous. The production design should help us know that.

Notation
A slash (/) indicates where the next line starts to overlap.

And Generally
We bring our blood-filled, smelly, hungry bodies with us everywhere we go. Bodies want things and remember things but bodies don't really understand what they want and remember. That is the task of the heart and the furious mind. As you work, do keep the body in mind as our characters' hearts and minds work so furiously to articulate themselves.

Avoid easy morality. Avoid villains, and heroes. And don't let the pace go slack.

An enemy must be worthy.
　　—Joy Harjo

LOVE

2018
Penelope and Vanessa

A café. Vanessa sits and fiddles on her phone. She wears sunglasses and sips a huge tea. Something about her puts you off. After a while, Penelope rushes in.

PENELOPE. Vee! Hey! Thank you for waiting, sorry I'm so late. Wow, you look—

Vee doesn't look well.

The same. The exact same.

VANESSA. You look the same except older. Hi.

If they hug, it's awkward.

PENELOPE. I'm going to grab a coffee. Do you want another tea? I'm assuming caffeine is still the one substance you don't put in your body—

VANESSA. I'm actually sober, so.

PENELOPE. Oh! Great! I'm—not.

VANESSA. You probably don't need to be.

PENELOPE. I know, sorry, I don't know why I said that, it was a little, um—can I get you another tea?

VANESSA. I'm all set.

PENELOPE. You sure?

VANESSA. I'm good.

PENELOPE. Okay.

Penelope starts to go get coffee, then—

Thank you for working around my schedule. I'm embarrassed we had to reschedule so much—but my hospital hours, plus the boys—

VANESSA. It's / fine.

PENELOPE. It's a Rubik's Cube.

VANESSA. It's fine.

PENELOPE. Let me get my—can you believe *Otis* working for the *mayor*? Did you see this? I saw him give a statement on TV the other day about—something. Children, probably? But, there he was, up there in a—suit. I felt like a "proud mom."

VANESSA. No, I didn't see that.

PENELOPE. No no no, sure.
Thank you for reaching out. Your voicemail was touching.

VANESSA. I enjoyed reestablishing our connection, too.

PENELOPE. And intriguing! Vee, I'm intrigued! Let me get my drugs and you can fill me in, okay?

VANESSA. Great.

PENELOPE. Not really drugs. / Caffeine.

VANESSA. Take your time.

PENELOPE. No, I'm gonna rush. I'm gonna rush because I am in *suspense*!

Pause.

What are we meeting about?

VANESSA. Otis. I want to talk to you about Otis.

2004
Penelope and Otis

The office of ArtStart, a scrappy nonprofit that paints murals with kids around New York. Penelope and Otis are not within arm's reach of one another for this scene. They're giddy.

PENELOPE. If you're so good at it, *you* do it!

OTIS. You need to learn how to do this.

PENELOPE. Do I?

OTIS. Absolutely.

PENELOPE. Or do you just *hate* doing it. So you're making *me* do it, under the guise of—

OTIS. / no.

PENELOPE. —*mentorship*. You have nowhere to be all day, *you* do / it.

OTIS. I do have somewhere to be.

PENELOPE. I'm looking at the calendar!

OTIS. I'm getting a haircut.

PENELOPE. You don't want to fire him because you hate being the bad guy. Admit it!

OTIS. I do hate it but / that's not why—

PENELOPE. Ha! / See?

OTIS. —that's *not* why I'm making you do it. I know how to do it. I've done it. You don't. You haven't. I'm giving you—a gift.

PENELOPE. You're giving me a gift.

OTIS. Yes.

PENELOPE. Literally the most ridiculous thing I've ever heard in my life.

OTIS. There's a playbook. Everything professional has a playbook.

PENELOPE. It's like breaking up with someone. It *is* breaking up with / someone—

OTIS. Listen. / *Listen.*

PENELOPE. Why pretend there's a nice way to do it?

OTIS. There's not a *nice* way to do it, there's a *right* way to do it. You have to do this, I'm making you do this. Wing it, if you want, that's fine. I suggest you listen to someone who's done it before and see what you learn.

PENELOPE. Okay I'll listen you're a fucking coward but fine I'm listening, hi.

Charmed, Otis cracks up and loses focus.

Hello. Where is this *incredible* advice I'm supposed to be receiving?

OTIS. *(Composure regained.)* Look him in the eye, the whole time.

PENELOPE. Otis, he's older than me.

OTIS. Repeat after me. Look him in the eye.

PENELOPE. Look him in the eye.

OTIS. Do *not* apologize.

PENELOPE. Do not apologize.

OTIS. You're not sorry.

PENELOPE. I'm not sorry because I'm a capitalist robot. *(Robot voice.)* "You are terminated."

OTIS. *(Cracking up a little.)* If you're sorry, you're making a mistake. You're not. This is *his* mistake. Do not go through this like you're the one who made the mistake.

PENELOPE. I am not repeating that.

OTIS. Be blunt, be clear.

He gestures.

PENELOPE. Be blunt, be clear, be *not* sorry, look him right in the eye.

She notices something on her computer.

Oh my god he *just* emailed us. Like right this second. Otis. We *summoned* him.

She scans the email.

He wants to come in, about—oh, just the shirts. The kids' T-shirts.

OTIS. *("Focus.")* Penelope.

PENELOPE. Sorry.

OTIS. Last thing, and this one is going to be hard for you: Do not fill the silence. Don't be afraid of silence. Say what you have to say, and wait.

PENELOPE. Why will that be hard for me?

OTIS. Because you're a fucking chatterbox.

Penelope pretends she's offended.

Which most of the time is very charming.

PENELOPE. Oh good.

OTIS. But it's not helpful for this.

PENELOPE. *(Teasing.)* Oh no?

OTIS. No. Once you've made your point, *stop talking*. Like this.
> *Long, long pause during which they get to stare at one another, unfettered. Someone smiles. Someone smiles back.*

Okay?

PENELOPE. Okay.

2018
Penelope and Jamie

Penelope and Jamie's apartment. Penelope is eating a late dinner. Jamie is here too, cleaning up. He ate earlier.

JAMIE. More lamb?

> *Jamie comes to get her plate. She's distracted.*

You good or can I take this?

PENELOPE. Oh. I'm good.
It was really good babe, thank you.

JAMIE. The boys hated it. Of course.

> *Pause.*

Dude. You okay?

PENELOPE. I had coffee with Vanessa Schaeffer* today.

JAMIE. Who?

PENELOPE. Vee.

> *He's still confused.*

Lap dance.

JAMIE. Oh shit! How is *she* doing?

PENELOPE. Uh, *she* thinks she's doing well. I thought she seemed pretty fragile but.
She's sober and vegan and, you know. *Mindful*.

JAMIE. Is she still wearing S and M gear to teach young children?

PENELOPE. *("About that.")* Yeah.

---

* Feel free to change Vanessa's last name to suit the ethnicity of the Vanessa actress.

JAMIE. No, really?

PENELOPE. No, but it's funny you mention that. She's part of a group. Of women. She's *leading* a group of women who are speaking to the *New York Times* about Otis.

JAMIE. Harrington? *Our* Otis?

PENELOPE. They're "coming forward."

JAMIE. About what?

PENELOPE. Workplace harassment. Sexual misconduct. That kind of...
Marissa, too.

JAMIE. Marissa...

PENELOPE. Eve's old roommate.* She had my job before me?

JAMIE. Right right right.

PENELOPE. Shit. What if Marissa talked to Eve, and Eve said something to our *parents*?

Jamie just looks at her.

My dad was against that job from the—you know? I'll like, never hear the end of it.

JAMIE. Oh, man. Have you talked to him?

PENELOPE. My dad?

JAMIE. *Otis.*

PENELOPE. Oh, no. No.

JAMIE. You should call him. Does he know?

PENELOPE. Dunno.

JAMIE. Did you tell her? About you and Otis?

Penelope winces.

PENELOPE. I said I wasn't at liberty to speak because the Mayor's Office allocates funds to the hospital.

JAMIE. What?

PENELOPE. I know.

JAMIE. That doesn't make any sense.

---

* Eve is Penelope's sister.

PENELOPE. *(Laughing, embarrassed.)* I know!

JAMIE. Wow. Fuck.

Do you—

Are you—

Man. Are you…

Pause.

PENELOPE. Am I what?

JAMIE. Are you on her side or his?

She looks at him.

Or—their side. Are you on their side or his?

She keeps looking at him.

2004
Penelope and Jamie

Jamie's messy bedroom. Penelope and Jamie are reading in bed. Jamie reads Parallel Lives *by Phyllis Rose; Penelope reads* Bush at War *by Bob Woodward. They had sex pretty recently.*

JAMIE. Hey, listen to this. "Jane panicked. She had been misunderstood. The love she bore Thomas was sisterly. Delightful but not impassioned enough—

Jamie's flip phone chirps with an incoming text. He checks it with some annoyance and decides not to respond.

"Delightful but not impassioned enough to reconcile her to the burdens of marriage. She would be his friend but they would never marry.

Another text.

"But this misunderstanding was the turning point in their relationship."

And another. He looks at the phone, tempted. Penelope observes him.

PENELOPE. You're not gonna check that?

JAMIE. Nah.

PENELOPE. Could be important.

JAMIE. *(Pointed.)* "This misunderstanding was the turning point in their relationship."

PENELOPE. I'll check it.

> *She reaches across him and snatches his phone.*

JAMIE. Dude, listen!

PENELOPE. I'm listening. Muriel? Muriel from J.E.? Really? *Muriel?*

> *He steals his phone back.*

JAMIE. What, she's cool.

PENELOPE. She's *fine*.

JAMIE. I mean, she's fairly high status, no?

PENELOPE. Sure.
I mean, she's not like, *girlfriend material* but.

JAMIE. You're not even listening.

PENELOPE. Of course I am. The misunderstanding was the turning point in their relationship.

> *Okay, she was listening. She gloats. He concedes.*
> *As he goes back to reading—*

I'm sleeping with my boss.

JAMIE. Wait really?

PENELOPE. Yeah.

JAMIE. Otis?

PENELOPE. Yeah.

> *Pause.*

Sorry, you were saying.

JAMIE. Um.
"For the words *love* and *marriage* had been spoken. And while she rejected the marriage, she had now conceived it. And no matter how impossible a thing appears, once it can be imagined, it can be enacted."

PENELOPE. Ooo, I love that. No matter how impossible a thing appears…what is it?

JAMIE. Once it can be imagined, it can be enacted.

PENELOPE. *Im*possibility implies *pos*sibility.

JAMIE. Yes. Yes!

PENELOPE. It's like, the big leap on the number line, the *greatest leap* on the number line isn't *zero to one*. It's—not knowing there *is* a number line, and then realizing you're on it, at zero. The greatest leap is—nothing to zero.

She's pleased with this. So is he.

What made you pick up Phyllis Rose?

JAMIE. Because—

Another text pulls his attention.

I'm making my way down…my mom's…

PENELOPE. Right right right. Your mom's syllabus.

Pause.

What does *Muriel* have to say about it?

JAMIE. She's angry.

PENELOPE. What did you do.

JAMIE. Well, apparently, canceling dinner plans day of is, and I quote, "unacceptable unless a close family member died."

PENELOPE. You were supposed to have dinner with her tonight?

JAMIE. *Tentatively.*

Another text. He checks it.

Man, cell phones are fucking weird. Look what she just called me.

PENELOPE. *(Squinting to read his screen.)* A—"missed abortion opportunity," oh god.

JAMIE. She would *never* say that to my face. She doesn't say anything to my face.

He puts the phone away for good.

The greatest leap is nothing to zero. That's great.

PENELOPE. It's cool you're reading your mom's syllabus.

JAMIE. It was Alissa's idea but our mom is so psyched, it's adorable.

PENELOPE. I want to join your book club.

JAMIE. You should.
PENELOPE. I will.

> *They both go back to reading.*

How *old* is Otis?

PENELOPE. Nineteen years older than us.

JAMIE. Forty-*two*? Shit! He looks good but that is *old*.

PENELOPE. Remember when Zoe Drysdale was sleeping with Professor Crane?

JAMIE. Oh, yeah. Baffling.

PENELOPE. *Baffling*. This isn't *that*, right?

JAMIE. *No.*

PENELOPE. Right? Okay. Great.

> *They keep reading.*

JAMIE. Isn't he married?

PENELOPE. Otis? Um. Yes.

JAMIE. Do they have kids?

PENELOPE. No. Not yet.

JAMIE. Damn, girl.

PENELOPE. It feels like I'm following him off a cliff. It's awesome.

> *Penelope goes back to reading for about one second.*

Don't tell anyone, okay?

JAMIE. Sure.

PENELOPE. Seriously. Like, you might think it's fine to tell Alissa on the train or whatever, but you don't know if his *wife* is on that train, or—someone else they know? You now have information that can *ruin* his life. That's a big responsibility. I'm trusting you.

> *To Jamie that actually is a revelation.*

JAMIE. Totally. Got it.

> *They read a bit more.*

So what's it like?

PENELOPE. Sleeping with Otis? It's great.

They keep reading.

JAMIE. What's great about it?

PENELOPE. He's a grown-up.

2004
Penelope and Otis

The ArtStart office. Penelope is on a call. Across the office, Otis is engrossed in something on his computer.

PENELOPE. Yes, *hi.* I'm calling to check on the final enrollment for the mural this Saturday? We have eight confirmed, which is great, but maybe three more are joining? Uh, Jalen Rivera, Rachel Prosper, and Magic Owens?

Right. So, if we go over eight, we need to send an additional teaching artist.

For safety, for fun, and it's an insurance requirement.

Yeah.

Should I just make those calls myself?

Not at all. I'll do it right now and let you know. Is it better to reach you by phone or email, Sherry? Great. Thanks. You too. Thanks. Bye.

She hangs up.

That woman is so sweet but I'm like, who put her in *charge*?! Every little thing requires ten follow-up calls and I just end up doing it anyway. Did you take the Benjamin Moore order over to Groundswell?

Pause.

OTIS. What?

PENELOPE. The Groundswell mural that starts on Saturday. Did you drop off the supplies?

OTIS. Oh. Yes. On—Monday.

PENELOPE. Wonderful. What did you forget?

OTIS. What did I forget.

PENELOPE. It starts with an "s" and ends with a "preadsheet."

OTIS. I forgot to mark the delivery on the spreadsheet. I'm sorry.

PENELOPE. No problem.

She tries to keep working but a strange energy from him is distracting her.

Are you—watching a movie?

OTIS. Kind of.

PENELOPE. What does that mean?

OTIS. Come and have a look.

PENELOPE. Seriously?

Pause.

I have to call Jalen Rivera's mother.

OTIS. Do that in a minute.

PENELOPE. I should do it now.

OTIS. Okay. If you're sure.

PENELOPE. I'm sure.

OTIS. Okay.

Penelope starts to call Jalen Rivera's mother but hangs up mid-dial. She's intrigued by Otis's activity across the room but feels shy about going to investigate.

Eventually she crosses to peek at his computer screen.

She's shocked.

PENELOPE. Aren't you afraid?

OTIS. Of what?

Pause.

PENELOPE. Search history?

OTIS. I delete it.

PENELOPE. I'm like so terrified "delete search history" is a lie.

OTIS. What are you searching for that needs deleting?

Pause.

Come here.

She looks around, tempted yet timid.

PENELOPE. I thought we said not in the office. Anyone could walk in.

OTIS. Vee is at PS 84. No trainings today.

PENELOPE. Your wife comes in to print sometimes.

OTIS. Rebecca's at work.

He stands, moves to a window where he can see the sidewalk.

I'll look out.

He gestures to the chair he just vacated.
Penelope takes a seat. This isn't the first time she's watched porn, but it's the first time she's done it with someone else.

What do you want to do?

PENELOPE. What do you want me to do?

OTIS. I want you to put your hand somewhere.

She doesn't for a long moment. Then—she almost does.

Do you want to touch yourself?

PENELOPE. I don't know.

OTIS. Try it and see.

She tries it for a bit. It's scary, exciting, fun.

PENELOPE. Okay. I did it.

OTIS. You don't want to keep going?

She glances towards the door.

PENELOPE. I'm scared of someone coming in.

OTIS. I'm looking out.

She starts masturbating more, now with the intention of finishing. At first she stays with herself. Eventually she glances back at Otis. They catch eyes.

He goes to her. He plays with her hair as she continues.

PENELOPE. You are *not* looking out.

OTIS. So you better finish quick.

She masturbates harder, better. She closes her eyes.

A loud clanking noise at the front door makes her scream. She pushes the power button on the monitor so hard it knocks the monitor off the table.

Otis, unperturbed, checks the window.

That was the mailman. That was the mailman putting mail in our mailbox.

PENELOPE. No that was the *Universe* giving us a *warning.*

She goes for the fallen computer.

OTIS. Leave it.

PENELOPE. I'm not, um—there anymore. My heart is pounding!

OTIS. Alright then.

Take it from the top.

He goes back to the window.

PENELOPE. You mean…

OTIS. You need to start over, start over.

PENELOPE. I broke your computer.

OTIS. It's *our* computer, and it's okay.

PENELOPE. Okay…

She returns to the chair. She starts to start over.

OTIS. Turn around and look at me. I want to see your beautiful face when you come.

Penelope turns to face him.

2018
Penelope and Otis

A bar. Penelope is giving Otis bad news.

PENELOPE. Vee. Marissa. Whitney. And a girl I've never heard of.

OTIS. Megan?

Penelope looks at him. Who the fuck is Megan?

PENELOPE. No. It was more—unique.

Pause.

OTIS. Keilynn?

PENELOPE. Keilynn. Yes.

OTIS. What about "Penelope"? Is she—joining the—

PENELOPE. Movement? Dude. You slept with *all* of them?

OTIS. Not slept with but.

PENELOPE. What does that mean?

OTIS. I drew the line at intercourse.

Pause.

PENELOPE. Was it during—
Was it the same time period as us?

OTIS. Maybe. One or two.

PENELOPE. Which "one or two"?

OTIS. Does it matter?

PENELOPE. Yes, it does.

OTIS. I'm not positive, it was a while ago but.

PENELOPE. *But.* Vee?

He nods.

Marissa?

OTIS. Not during the same time as us, no.

PENELOPE. Is that why she stopped working for you?

OTIS. I didn't think so. We hung out a few times after she quit, so.

PENELOPE. You hung out.

OTIS. Yeah.

PENELOPE. Did you, um—
Did you love them?

OTIS. No.

PENELOPE. Did you *tell* them you loved them?

OTIS. No.

PENELOPE. Not a single one. Not once. Not once did you—grease the wheels with—with—star-crossed—

OTIS. No, Pen.

PENELOPE. —*love?*

OTIS. No.

Pause.

PENELOPE. How much does Rebecca know?

OTIS. Nothing, as far as I know but.

PENELOPE. Is that possible? Can you live with a man drawing the line at intercourse with five women and know *nothing*?

OTIS. I don't know, Pen. Lots of things I knew are turning out to be—

PENELOPE. Did you call them / too?

OTIS. —wrong, what?

PENELOPE. Last Thanksgiving. After those stories started coming out in the news, and you called me, for the first time in—
Did you call them, too? Did you call all of them, too?

OTIS. No. Just you.

PENELOPE. Why just me.

OTIS. Because. You and I are—

PENELOPE. Because you knew what my answer would be.
And you knew what theirs would be.

OTIS. I called *you* because you and I are friends.
Is your answer the same?
Is your answer to my question the same?

PENELOPE. Is my answer to your question the same. Otis. Are you going to *say sorry*?

OTIS. I'm sorry.
I'm sorry.
What are you going to do?

PENELOPE. I love you.

OTIS. You do?

> *Pause.*

PENELOPE. I don't know what I'm going to do.

> *Otis looks down. Penelope reaches across the table and takes his hand. They stay like this a moment. She pulls her hand away.*

2018
Penelope and Ron

A desk at the New York Times. *A recording device on the table is turned off.*

Penelope looks on, uncomfortable but stoic, as Ron reads over his hand-scribbled notes.

RON. The details vary but the patterns are—patterns. All young, attractive female hires.

PENELOPE. I don't know about *all* attractive.

Ron looks up.

RON. Lots of after-work outings to bars. Paid for by the boss. Rounds of shots. Paid for by the boss.

PENELOPE. I can see how what you're doing is easier if you call him "the boss." He has a name.

RON. Otis Harrington.

PENELOPE. I brought a thank-you note I saved from one of the foster kids we worked with.

RON. Great.

PENELOPE. Have you ever had a job where you get thank-you notes from kids?

RON. No. He always tells a story, an icebreaker, early on, about an ex-girlfriend or ex-wife that—involves—
Sex and her body. The *attractiveness* of her body. The stories include her measurements. Her bra size. Her— *(Squinting at his handwriting.)* Athletic history.

PENELOPE. And I guess these stories were—titillating? Or, gross?

RON. I think it's safe to say they were intended to be titillating. Testing the waters.

PENELOPE. Aren't we coming for the men who *don't* test the waters?

RON. The point is the pattern. Five different women, same situation. Young. Inexperienced in the workplace. Hired to manage the office and within a year, year and a half, their clothes are off. They've all come forward.

PENELOPE. I have not come forward.

RON. Another woman spoke to me, after you and I emailed.

PENELOPE. Megan?

He can't answer that.

Whatever. He told me in his neighborhood—when he was a kid—in the yard between the towers, he saw a woman tied to a tree—this was during the daytime—a woman tied to a tree, naked, and lots of different men had sex with her, one after the other. And she was screaming and laughing, screaming and laughing. And he and his friends were at home, watching through the window—they were like *eight*—and they were laughing too. At this naked woman tied to a tree. He said, "the '70s were a crazy time."

RON. If you're saying his—

PENELOPE. I shouldn't say "woman" she was a *girl*. No one framed this for them. No one taught them to see what they were looking at. Rape. People—adults—walked right by.

RON. If you're saying his upbringing is *relevant*—

PENELOPE. And I shouldn't say "men," either! She was a *girl* and her rapists were *boys*. The only adults in the story are the—bystanders.

RON. If you're saying his upbringing is relevant, I agree. If you're saying it's an *excuse* / I don't.

PENELOPE. I'm saying, the first story he told me about sex wasn't titillating, it was tragic.

Pause.

I am not speaking on the record. Is that clear? Nothing I said goes in your story.

RON. Are you ready to? Speak on the record? *(Gesturing to the recording device.)* May I?

PENELOPE. I'm not here to go on the record. I'm here to—disrupt it.

RON. You can't disrupt it by staying quiet.

PENELOPE. I can get to you. I can *try* to get to you. You're going to write what you're going to write, I guess, but I *could* make you—lose a little sleep tonight.

RON. What am I losing sleep about?

PENELOPE. You're demonizing a human being! You're changing a person into a *demon* so your morality tale can end with his execution by the—internet firing squad. And everyone can go, "Aahh justice! We slayed the demon!" and get back to their—*juice cleanse*. But you *should* feel bad, Ron. You and your lazy readers who hate whoever the internet tells them to. Jesus. He used to drive kids home across multiple boroughs, when their parents couldn't pick them up, so they could do the program. He taught his little brothers to read. He taught *me* to *speak up*. The way I'm talking to you right now? Not scared or *grateful* that a man from the *New York Times* is paying attention to me? Not polite—you know how polite I used to be? *Always?* Always! To people who were *horrible* to me. Do you know where I learned there's *another option*? Not my parents' house or my ancestors in _____.* Not a gender studies class or a fucking Beyoncé video. It was Otis Harrington. *He* is the one who unleashed this woman who will not smile and nod while you teach her how to see her life. He is not perfect but he's done a lot of good in the world, more than most. He has hurt people but there is a lot of love in his heart, more than most. He is not someone to purge. Using him to purge *your* shame is cowardly. I think you're a coward.

RON. My shame about what?

PENELOPE. Dude, what were you writing about before my victim-hood started trending?

RON. In the course of this work, I've noticed a tendency to blame the people adjacent to the abusers as much as, or more than, the abusers themselves. I'm curious about that.

> *Pause.*

One woman said in an email that at the time she felt flattered but in hindsight she feels she was *lured*. She felt she had been hired for her *appeal*—to his *appetite* and her time at ArtStart was a "steady erosion of my professionalism with increasingly less subtle advances until he got what he really hired me for."

---

* Name the country/region of the Penelope actress's ancestors.

PENELOPE. Increasingly less subtle advances.

He looks up at her.

Seduction. I accepted those advances, eagerly. Twenty-two-year-old girls have appetites too.

RON. Penelope. If you felt something they didn't, say it. Say it! Please! The story needs you!

PENELOPE. The story...needs me?

Pause.

Oh. You don't—have it, do you. Not quite.

She waits for confirmation that doesn't come.

You don't have a story. Otis is not—famous. And these women, they don't want to— *(Glances at the recorder.)* talk about their *bodies* in the *New York Times. I* don't, why would they? That's why you kept calling *me*. Because you don't have what you need to, uh—
And maybe you don't have it because—it's not really a story.

RON. A man, the only one with the power to hire, fire, and dispense salaries, exclusively hires women in a work environment which converts them from young professionals to sexual entities for his own enjoyment.

PENELOPE. In my case, you'd have to change *his* enjoyment to *our* enjoyment.

RON. You don't find the *pattern* disturbing? *Five* women. You make six, that I know of?

PENELOPE. So you assassinate someone in your paper whenever you feel disturbed?

RON. The real power of the press is the power to deem a story *news*. You're right, some editors would not find this strong enough. But. If this movement is going to be thorough—if this movement is going to *happen*—I believe his transgressions must be named. He exclusively hires women twenty years younger—

PENELOPE. It was a starter job.

RON. Only females?

PENELOPE. We taught *children art*. How many male art teachers did you have, Ron? If I walk out there, how many male office managers will I find?

RON. He gets them drunk.

PENELOPE. We drank together, yes. Was twenty-two your sober year? Was forty-two?

RON. He complains about his marriage.

PENELOPE. His marriage sucks.

RON. And jokes that he's a feminist so you don't have to wear a bra to work.

PENELOPE. And *that* is fucked. I never heard him say that but that—sounds like him. But the *New York Times*, Ron? Really? He's devoted his career to kids no one's looking out for. And—okay you cannot put this in your story but—Otis is a generous, creative lover. I know the age difference is supposedly this big power thing but—Ron, listen. Sex with guys in their twenties is a soul-crushing, orgasm-faking *disaster*.

Ron chuckles.

RON. Can I quote you on that?

PENELOPE. No.

RON. Anonymously?

PENELOPE. *(Laughing with him.)* No!

Pause.

Did someone tell you they didn't consent? Did anyone make allegations of, um—

RON. Assault?

PENELOPE. Yeah.

RON. No.
They all say they consented, though Vanessa Schaeffer questions what "consent" really means in that structure, and so do I.
Either way: Otis rolled out his tried-and-true tactics with young women he had very real power over. Again and again.
My wife says it's like Bobby Fischer inviting you to play chess, pretending he's never heard of the game.

Pause.

At the time, did you know you weren't the only one he'd—
Had relations with? At your office?

> *Pause.*

PENELOPE. No, I didn't.
And I feel hurt. But not—exploited.

RON. *(Gently.)* Well, that's fortunate. They refer to themselves as victims.

PENELOPE. That is—hard to hear.
I am not his victim. My story is not theirs but I can't—*say that*—because no one will hear me. My story's already been written by everyone else: I'm either his victim or his slut.
You think you're doing noble work, I see that, but.
I don't trust you to teach people how to see me.
And I don't trust you to teach them how to see Otis Harrington.

RON. He is an admirable person in many respects. In my opinion, in one crucial respect, he is despicable. This *is* a complicated story, not obviously newsworthy. That's exactly why it must be written. Men do what he does all the time, all over the world, and they get to hide under a blanket of anonymity. "Good men" who think it's A-okay to use the workplace as their own personal sexual shopping mall.

> *Penelope balks at this.*

You don't trust me, I see that. Pretend you do for the next half hour and see how you feel.

> *He gestures to the recorder.*

Then, if you want to withdraw, you can. Before you leave here today.

PENELOPE. How many of the others are willing to name themselves?

RON. Two.

PENELOPE. How many do you need to run the story?

RON. Three.

PENELOPE. Ah. So it's not just my complications you're after.

> *He shrugs—true enough.*
> *And perhaps for the first time, Penelope specifically imagines inserting herself into the story. This might take a moment.*

I'm thinking about—the hospital director.

RON. Sure.

PENELOPE. My co-residents.

RON. Yeah. I get it.

PENELOPE. My *patients*, who have a hard enough time going under for a surgeon with "*such cute dimples.*"* My *father.* They'll all read it and the next time they look at me, they'll see a twenty-two-year-old on her knees.

When you write about me, you're going to describe the color of my hair.

RON. Go on the record now, and I can go back to the others and see if you naming yourself empowers them to do the same. If one of them comes around, you can revert to anonymity. Or even— drop out of the story.

PENELOPE. Nice, bro.

RON. Getting this story right is the right thing to do. There's no shame being strategic about it.

PENELOPE. His son was the youngest baby I ever held, till my own.

She stands.

Enjoy the rest of your day, Ron.

He stands with her.

RON. Shit. Okay. Well, thank you for coming in. If you wake up in the middle of the night and want to give the truth a chance, call me. Anytime. I enjoyed our conversation.

As he riffles for a card, he sets papers aside. She picks one up. It's a picture of Marvin the Martian.

PENELOPE. Marvin the Martian.

RON. Your former boss is a big fan.

PENELOPE. I *know.*

RON. It refers to a tattoo. As an image for the story I thought it might be—

An unexpected detail can be—enlivening.

---

* Or another description of the actress's appearance, e.g. "such exotic eyes," "those wonderful curls," etc. The description should be a compliment only a woman would get and disrespectful to a surgeon.

33

PENELOPE. But you're not allowed to write about the *tattoo*.
Who told you about it? You never said you spoke about me, specifically. Aren't you *obligated* to—confirm, or—yeah, *confirm* it *exists*?
Isn't that like—
Fact checking?

    Pause.

RON. *You* have a Marvin the Martian tattoo?

    Penelope freezes. Then—

    She speeds up her exit, whether that's zipping up her coat or putting her purse over her shoulder or rushing to the door. Whatever. She needs to get the fuck out of here.

PENELOPE. Otis is not the enemy. You are *not* taking down the enemy.

RON. You're right. He's not the enemy. He's a friend.
And we're holding a friend accountable.
Don't you think we owe that to our friends?

2018
Penelope, Vanessa, and Whitney

    Vee's apartment. Whitney, Vanessa, and Penelope are having tea. Whitney and Vanessa are laughing.

WHITNEY. For a bonus I got a TV! / A freaking TV!

VANESSA. Ha! *God.* That is so him.

WHITNEY. Any word from Marissa?

VANESSA. No. The trains are probably fucked.

WHITNEY. Anyway. Yeah. He gets me this *massive* TV, the *last, new* TV that wasn't a flat screen, it was like a—a—*treasure chest.*

    She laughs.

Of course I get my "bonus" the day before TV technology makes a hard right.

VANESSA. Okay, ready for this? He paid my *rent*. Mm-hmm. For two months. *Two months.*

WHITNEY. Wow. *Wow.*

PENELOPE. Was that when Jenny's boyfriend stole the rent money?

VANESSA. Uh, yes, actually.

PENELOPE. I remember that. *(To Whitney, re: Vee.)* Her roommate's boyfriend was so shady. Vee was so upset. *(To Vee.)* Remember? And the next day, we blew off work and went to that board games bar and played—nondominant-hand Pictionary.

Pause.

VANESSA. I don't remember that.

PENELOPE. It was nice.

Pause.

So, Otis paying your rent was—

Penelope looks at them.
They look at Penelope.

Diminishing. Obvi / ously.

VANESSA. *Very* / diminishing.

WHITNEY. Completely.

PENELOPE. Sure. Sure.

Pause. Vanessa checks her phone. Still no update from Marissa.

VANESSA. Marissa and Ryan got married, did you see / that?

PENELOPE. No. Wow. Finally.

VANESSA. I wasn't invited. How's Jamie?

PENELOPE. He's great.

WHITNEY. *(To Vanessa, re: Marissa; nervous.)* She's not—bailing, is she?

VANESSA. *(Firm but low volume, eager to reassure Whitney but not wanting Penelope to sense the story is fragile.)* No. No.

The subtext here is, if Marissa bails, not just on the night but the story, Vanessa doesn't just need one more woman to go on the record, she needs two, which puts more pressure on Whitney.

WHITNEY. Okay.

> *Pause.*

PENELOPE. *(To Whitney.)* Are you gonna—do the story?

WHITNEY. I—
haven't decided.

> *Pause.*

I totally totally totally *might*.

> *Pause.*

VANESSA. We used to watch the uh, *The Bang Bus* together. Did you watch that with him?

WHITNEY. Oh my god *The BANG BUS!* *(To Penelope.)* Did you guys watch that?

PENELOPE. Uhhh what's the—*Bang Bus*?

VANESSA. *(To Penelope.)* Well, you know how Otis *loves* porn.

> *The briefest pause to clock Penelope—will she confirm?*

There was this website, *The Bang Bus*. And—and—

WHITNEY. And in *The Bang Bus*, these guys drive around in a van—

> *Whitney and Vanessa tag team telling this. It should be loose and interrupty but do lift the details of the porn—every one of those details is the point of the story.*

VANESSA. These *not cute* guys.

WHITNEY. These ugly guys / drove around—

VANESSA. Not ugly! Average. Ugly would be more interesting.

WHITNEY. Yes. These very average white guys drive around and pick up a girl—

VANESSA. A hot girl.

WHITNEY. Mm she's *basic*. And she's walking the streets of Florida alone!
They offer her a ride. She gets in—

VANESSA. 'Cause *that's* a thing.

WHITNEY. Totally. They make small talk. And then one of them says something like…

VANESSA. "Can we see your tits?"

WHITNEY. But like, so nice and sweet. "Can we see your tits?"

Whitney and Vanessa crack up.

VANESSA. And she *resists*, she's *shy*. They go back and forth and back and forth. I actually think *that's* the pornography. The gradual, like…

WHITNEY. wearing down.

VANESSA. Exactly. But, sure enough, eventually she takes off all her clothes, she's like really turned on, and, boom. Everybody's bangin'.

Pause.

My therapist calls it the eroticization of female reluctance.
(To Penelope.) You never watched that with him?

Penelope shakes her head.

WHITNEY. Oh but at the end! The end is the special part.

VANESSA. The end is / very special.

WHITNEY. When they're done, they kick her out of the van, leave her by the side of the road, and drive away laughing. They roll down the window so she can *hear* them laughing.

Pause.

VANESSA. And Otis laughed, too.

Pause.

WHITNEY. So did I.

VANESSA. *(Releasing Whitney from feeling complicit.)* Well, sure. You were having fun together.
Do *we* do that? *Can* we do that? Fuck someone who we also *mock*?

WHITNEY. Maybe. Some girl somewhere does.

Pause.

PENELOPE. Good for her.

VANESSA. Good for her.

WHITNEY. He took me to this club? This like *Russian* club in—

VANESSA. *(Squealing with recognition.)* Bensonhurst!

WHITNEY. *(Cracking up.)* Bensonhurst! Oh my god who goes to / Bensonhurst?

VANESSA. Right? No chance of bumping into anyone we knew. Oh my god that place. That *music*. That bartender!

WHITNEY. That bartender's BOOBS!

Whitney and Vanessa totally lose it laughing.

VANESSA. *(Gasping, through laughter.)* They were up to here! She was like—ninety years old.

WHITNEY. *(Also through laughter.)* I think she was like forty-five—she just smoked a lot.

VANESSA. *(Practically choking.)* I went down on him on the dance floor.

WHITNEY. Oh no! Sorry I'm laughing.

VANESSA. It's okay! It's okay!

Vanessa and Whitney keep laughing together for a strangely long time.

Watching their catharsis from the outside starts to unsettle Penelope.

WHITNEY. *(Settling down, wiping her eyes.)* Oh my god. How are you feeling?

PENELOPE. Me? I'm—listening.

Pause. Vanessa gets a text. She reads it.

VANESSA. *Fuck.*

Vanessa shows Whitney a text from Marissa. The text says Marissa is not coming tonight and is not joining the story. It's probably a fairly long message.

PENELOPE. Is everything okay?

Whitney is crushed. Vanessa and Whitney silently agree it's best not to share this with Penelope.

VANESSA. Yeah. It's fine. Marissa can't make it tonight. *(To Whitney.)* It's *fine.*

Pause.

PENELOPE. Vee, are you still painting?

VANESSA. Yeah. I'm a famous artist.

Pause.

WHITNEY. What about Megan?

VANESSA. Well, no, because they never… She never went there with him.

WHITNEY. Couldn't she like, talk about how he—was?

VANESSA. *(Pessimistic.)* Maybe.

Megan. Man, she never fell for any of his shit. She was like, "Why is he always talking about his old girlfriends? That is so inappropriate." She made me feel *really* bad for taking rent money, too. She like, yelled at me.

At the time I was like, what are you talking about, I'm *broke*. But.

WHITNEY. But she was right.

VANESSA. She was right. If he pays your rent…

> *Pause.*

PENELOPE. *(Genuine, confused.)* If he pays your rent what?

WHITNEY. He wins and you lose.

> *Pause.*

PENELOPE. Well, if Marissa's not coming, I do have an early procedure. Whitney, so great seeing you.

> *Whitney holds out her arms for a hug, to Penelope's surprise. They hug. It's nice, though it goes on longer than Penelope expects and she finds herself feeling suddenly maternal towards Whitney.*

WHITNEY. So good seeing you, Penelope.

PENELOPE. You too, Whitney.

> *In drawing back from their hug, Penelope sees tape and bandaging on Whitney's forearm. Does this suggest suicide?*

Are—

You—

Um. Are you okay, sweetie?

WHITNEY. I mean, honestly? I don't *know*! 'Cause like… He didn't love me. Duh. I know—haha—*now*. But like, do *any of them*? Or am I just like a *magnet* for like…

> *Pause. Whitney sees Penelope glance at the bandaging on her arm.*

Oh! You mean—

This is not—um—suicide. Haha. No, it's really not. I got a—tattoo removed. An embarrassing tattoo from my youth.

PENELOPE. *(She means this.)* Good for you.
Good for you.

Pause. Whitney is buoyed by Penelope's tenderness.

WHITNEY. I'm gonna do it.

PENELOPE. Do what?

WHITNEY. *(To Vanessa.)* I'll do it.

VANESSA. Really? Are you sure?

WHITNEY. Yeah.
I mean, it's hard, it's really hard but.

VANESSA. Are you kidding, it's a fucking nightmare. That's why coming forward is brave. Because it sucks.

Penelope watches them.

I am—
Wow.
I am so fucking proud of you.

2004
Penelope, Jamie, and Vanessa

A small falafel joint. Penelope and Jamie sit at a table, waiting for their order.

PENELOPE. Otis said a kind of amazing thing at work today. I had to fire this guy—I told you about this?

JAMIE. Yeah he made a—fat joke about a *kid*?

PENELOPE. Yeah. He made a fat joke and the program director heard. And Otis made me fire him.

Vanessa bursts in wearing a crazy outfit: black lingerie that is very visible under a rather see-through white vintage nightgown, and huge sunglasses. She looks pretty nuts.

VANESSA. What is *up* you guys?

PENELOPE. Vee! Hey! You're—here.

VANESSA. I saw you guys through the window. *Hey, Jamie.*

JAMIE. Hi, Vee. That is quite an outfit.

PENELOPE. Ew! Jamie stop being a creep. Sorry. He's a creep.

VANESSA. Not at all! It's a statement outfit and I appreesh the acknowledge!

JAMIE. She appreeshes the acknowledge. I'm not a creep.

PENELOPE. Here, take my seat, I have to go meet Eve anyway.

JAMIE. No, no, sit. Here.

He pulls up a chair for her.

VANESSA. Such a gentleman! This was my *grandmother's* nightgown. That she actually like, wore to sleep. How *fucking* amazing is that.

It takes a moment for them to realize this isn't rhetorical.

PENELOPE. That's amazing.   JAMIE. So incredible yeah.

VANESSA. She lived in Ohio, then she died, and when we went to her house, my sister and my mom were all, I want *this*, I want *that*. But all *I* wanted was this nightgown.

JAMIE. It's nice.

VANESSA. The night before she died she said, "Vanessa I know you've lost your way but I *believe* in you."
I was like, *who's* lost? Bitch, I am *found*! But I think that was a reaction to my eye makeup which was *very* goth at the time. The important thing is she said: I believe in you. And I was like, thanks Granma! And then she died!

JAMIE. I'm so sorry.   PENELOPE. Sorry for your loss.

VANESSA. Thanks! So now, whenever I wear it, I'm all wrapped up in: "I believe in you."

JAMIE. We all need an "I believe in you" nightgown.

VANESSA. I love him.

PENELOPE. I was just telling Jamie about having to fire Matt Becker and this thing Otis / said.

VANESSA. Wait, *you* fired him? Fuck! *I* wanted to fire him, but

Otis said he should do it. *(To Jamie.)* I slept with this teaching artist twice and he never called me once and then he said this really mean thing to a fat kid.

JAMIE. What a dick.

VANESSA. I love you.
So wait, *you* fired him?

PENELOPE. Yeah but Otis said this really smart thing while we were arguing about how to fire him. We were talking about how to do it, *when* to do it, *where* to do it, when the guy *emails*. And—

JAMIE. *(Standing.)* I'm totally listening, our food's up.

VANESSA. Get me a beer, Jamester?

JAMIE. Sure. Pen?

PENELOPE. I'm good.

He leaves.

I don't want to have to pee in the park.

VANESSA. Well *I* have been drinking since three and I am not done yet!

PENELOPE. Since three? But weren't you at—

VANESSA. Sh.

Vanessa burps. A pause.

PENELOPE. I'm seeing a show tonight with Eve and Marissa at the Bandshell.

VANESSA. I saw Tori there! She was *uh*-mazing, tell Marissa hi, what concert?

PENELOPE. Arcade Fire.

VANESSA. I don't know what that is.

Jamie comes back with two baskets of falafel sandwiches and two beers.

JAMIE. So, the guy you have to fire emails.

PENELOPE. Can you grab the hot sauce? Yeah, he emails.

JAMIE. About the incident?

PENELOPE. No. Which is—*pertinent*. He emails about something else but I was like, oh, he's coming in, I should fire him then. And

Otis says: No. Do *not* fire him when he comes for the shirts. He says—and this is what I wanted to tell you, I thought of you like, instantly. He said, *you have to give people their meeting.*

Pause. Vanessa and Jamie aren't as impressed as she wants.

Meaning: If he calls, to talk about—whatever's on *his* mind, as a boss you can't *hijack* that meeting and shove through your own agenda. That's—*irresponsible*. It's a "poor use of power." You have to give people their meeting. And if *you* have something to say, call your own meeting.

JAMIE. Oh.

PENELOPE. Kinda great right?

JAMIE. I can think of like eleven people at school who need this memo.

PENELOPE. Anyway. It made me think about our stuff.

VANESSA. Ooh! What's your *stuff*?

JAMIE. You know. Fights. And we—yeah. She's right.
We hijack each other's meetings a lot.

Penelope looks at him, surprised, happy.

VANESSA. What time is the concert?

PENELOPE. You're right I should go.

VANESSA. Say hi to Marissa for me. *(To Jamie.)* What do you guys fight about?

Penelope is reluctant to go.

PENELOPE. Did they change the hot sauce?

JAMIE. I don't know.

PENELOPE. It used to be creamier.

JAMIE. I think you're right.

PENELOPE. *(Heading out.)* Okay 'bye.

As Penelope leaves—

VANESSA. Bye "Pé"!
I call her "Pé." That's Penélope Cruz's nickname in Spain.

JAMIE. *(Laughing.)* Bye, Pé!

PENELOPE. *(To Jamie.)* Bye. Don't forget to, um. Hydrate.

2004
Penelope, Vanessa, and Rebecca

Penelope is at work in the ArtStart office. Rebecca, very pregnant, is printing a long document. They are together in silence for quite a while.

Vanessa comes in noisily, wearing the same crazy nightgown outfit from the last scene.

VANESSA. Oh my god, I'm so hungover. I had *sex* with *Jamie* last night.

PENELOPE. You—what?

VANESSA. Rebecca, oh my god! You look so huge and beautiful!

REBECCA. Hey, Vee.

VANESSA. I LOVE pregnant women! And I heard it's a *boy*! A tiny little Otis is swimming around in here, huh? Hey lil' guy, can't wait to meetcha! Okay, so Jamie and I stayed at Habib's forever, just like, *talking*... Then we hit up a second location—Irish dive bar—*classic*— and had a super special evening! Cosmos. Appletinis. Spicy waffle fries. Girl, he is an *amazing* listener. And he reads *books*, you know? Like, *books*? He's a *raging* feminist because his *mom* is this *super famous professor* of women's—something, of *us*, basically, so. Yeah. I wasn't gonna call it love at first sight because technically I have seen him before, but my heart was fluttering like a tiny little bird. By last call I felt so connected to him I would have sucked him off right there on the bar.

REBECCA. The printer's out of paper.

PENELOPE. It's on top of the file cabinets. Here I got it.

Penelope goes to reload the paper.

VANESSA. But I texted him last night to say I got home safe and then again this morning to say I'm sorry for breaking his chair and the window screen but I haven't heard a peep, of course, so *obviously* my feelings aren't mutual, as per yoosh. *(Like "usual.")* I mean, I'm sorry, I know he's your best friend but Pé. You should put a *warning label* on that guy. And it just hurts so much more when they're *nice*?

44

Like when it actually seems like they *care* about what you have to *say*? Fuck. I hate that I'm crying—but I *am*—because I'm hungover as shit, I'm getting my period tomorrow, and men are fucking *dicks*. How was the concert?

PENELOPE. Uh. Good.

VANESSA. *(Still crying.)* That's so awesome.

PENELOPE. *(Offering Vanessa a hug.)* Aw, sweetie. Come here.

> *As Vanessa goes into her arms, Penelope picks up a jar of ink.*
>
> *As they embrace, Penelope empties the bottle of ink all down the back of Vanessa's grandmother's nightgown. Her entire back is covered in jet-black ink.*

Oh my god, I'm so sorry! I had my calligraphy jar in my hand, I didn't realize it was open.

VANESSA. What?

PENELOPE. Don't move I'm so so sorry. Your dress. In the back. Let me get some paper towels. I'm such an *idiot*. Vee I am so sorry about your dress.

VANESSA. My dress? My dress?! *(Twisting around, checking the back of her nightgown.)* FUCK.

> *Vanessa hurries off, heading to the bathroom.*

AND IT'S *NOT* A DRESS!

> *Vanessa exits. A strange pause.*

REBECCA. It's not a dress?

PENELOPE. It's her grandmother's nightgown.

2004
Penelope and Otis

A cheesy club with Russian clientele in Bensonhurst. The music could be lowbrow Russian pop, or lowbrow American pop. Penelope sits alone at a cocktail table with two full drinks on it.

Penelope's flip phone rings. She sees who it is. Furious, she silences the call and downs one of the drinks. Then, she starts texting.

PENELOPE'S TEXTS.
can't talk bc I hate u

> *Penelope downs the other drink.*

V???!!!!

For real dude?

I can't believe you did that

She's awful

> JAMIE'S TEXTS.
> It WAS awful
>
> She gave me a lap dance for an hour
>
> AN HOUR

Really?

> Yeah she's been taking classes
>
> It was
>
> INTERMINABLE

Penelope laughs in spite of her rage and humiliation.

That was really inconsiderate

Seriously how could you do that?

                         I dunno she was down

You sleep with every girl who's down?

                         kinda?

Did you think about me at all?

Dude I work with her

She told the whole office

It was humiliating

                         humiliating for

                         you?

                         why?

Penelope is crying.

Otis comes back from the bar. (The way he doesn't reference her tears in the next few lines is kind.)

OTIS. Hi.
PENELOPE. Hi.
OTIS. Our drinks are all done.
PENELOPE. Sorry.
OTIS. That's okay.
PENELOPE. Can you get us more?
OTIS. Same thing?

PENELOPE. Yeah. But maybe a little bigger? Like *enormously huge* would be ideal.

OTIS. *(Chuckles.)* Okay.

Otis leaves. Penelope resumes texting.

PENELOPE'S TEXTS.
I can't do this anymore

My heart is breaking

It's broken

It's been broken for a long time

JAMIE'S TEXTS.
:(

Do you ever think about being with me?

Just me?

Pen we're 23

She stares at this. She doesn't know what to type.

Why didn't u tell me u were unhappy?

ok lets stop

I don't want to hurt you

We can just be best friends

I thought I was gonna have your cute fat babies

I never want to see you again

After a pause, the phone rings. She rejects the call.

don't call me ever again.

The phone rings again. She rejects it again.

I mean it.

Penelope throws her phone down and cries. It's off-putting and primal.

Otis returns with their enormously huge drinks. He sets them down. Pulls her to her feet. Gives her an enormously huge hug.

PENELOPE. Jamie doesn't want to be with me. He never did and he never will.

Otis just holds her as she cries. The hug might turn into a dance, maybe an old-fashioned kind of partner dance. Eventually, Penelope draws back and looks at him.

I'm thinking of deferring another year.

OTIS. Do they *let* you defer for a second year?

PENELOPE. Not from Stanford but one of the other schools, that offered me a full ride. They'll be more flexible. They want me more.

OTIS. A worse school.

PENELOPE. *(Pretty drunk.)* That is *very* subjective. There's a lot of, you know like, *hollow elitism* that I'm not sure translates into *actual* better placements.

OTIS. Penelope. Look at me.
If you don't quit I will fire you.
On Monday you're going to post an ad for your replacement.

She looks at him.

You don't belong at ArtStart and you know it.
I'm sorry. I was always rooting for you guys.

PENELOPE. *(Blows her nose.)* Okay fine I'll quit but I'm getting a tattoo of Marvin the Martian.
Because—
Well, I just am.
I hope that doesn't sound psycho.

A nice moment.

OTIS. Hey.

PENELOPE. What.

> *Pause.*

Say it.

OTIS. It's small but—you'll have an opinion.

PENELOPE. Oh. Okay.

OTIS. Jamie and I have plans to see *Spiderman* tomorrow night.

PENELOPE. I don't care.

OTIS. You don't care.

PENELOPE. Please cancel.

OTIS. Okay. That won't—
Give us away?

PENELOPE. Fine, go. Just don't become best friends with him. I mean, who cares whatever fuck that guy.

> *Pause.*

I thought you were going to tell me you loved me.

OTIS. I love you. You're going to go to California to learn to do incredible things.
And you'll take those things you learn and help people. You are going to save people's lives. You'll get thank-you notes from their kids. And when you do all of that, all of this will feel—small.

2009
Penelope and Otis

> *A bar. Penelope waits alone. Otis comes in with a beer and two shots. They're happy to see each other after a long time.*

PENELOPE. No! Otis, no. No shots. I'm *not* / drinking that!

OTIS. What / shots?

PENELOPE. I hate you.

OTIS. Oh, you mean *these* shots. / She *gave* them to us.

PENELOPE. God, you're a child. You're still a child! I ordered a *seltzer*. Where's my seltzer?

OTIS. Mm. Seltzer rots the liver.

Just one. We're celebrating!

PENELOPE. I'm scrubbing in for a kidney transplant in the morning!

OTIS. That's great!

PENELOPE. My first one!

OTIS. I told her we're celebrating your wedding and she insisted. It's not my fault!

PENELOPE. Yeah yeah, it's always the bartender's fault.

She rolls her eyes and takes the shot.

Happy?

OTIS. *(Holding up his shot.)* To you and Jamie. And yes, I am. I'm really happy, for you both.

He drinks, grabs the empty glasses and heads back to the bar.

Okay lemme grab your seltzer.

He exits. She laughs and shakes her head.

Otis returns with her seltzer—and two more shots.

PENELOPE. Dude. I'm serious.

OTIS. *(Re: the bartender.)* What can I say, she really likes you.

PENELOPE. Yeah, yeah. She *is* your type.

OTIS. Nah. She doesn't look a thing like you.

PENELOPE. Thank you, for the *decanter*.

Pause.

You guys sent us a crystal wine decanter and it's just lovely.

OTIS. Rebecca must have picked that out.

PENELOPE. No kidding.

OTIS. You're welcome.

PENELOPE. How is Rebecca?

OTIS. She's great.

PENELOPE. How's Max?

OTIS. Five!

PENELOPE. No!

OTIS. Right? He starts kindergarten in the fall.

PENELOPE. Wow. He's like, a person. Wow.

Pause.

OTIS. How's Jamie?

PENELOPE. He quit.

OTIS. Teaching?

PENELOPE. Yeah, sort of. He and a buddy started a consulting company together. They're off to a good start. I think. I'm not sure he can handle the freedom, but we'll see.

OTIS. What do you mean?

PENELOPE. He thrives with a little structure, I think? The entrepreneur thing is a whole different—I'm not sure it's his—nature. But. We'll see. I'm proud of him.

Pause.

OTIS. Good to see you.

PENELOPE. You, too.

They take the second shot.

2009
Jamie and Penelope

Penelope and Jamie's living room. Penelope is studying on the couch in her pajamas. Jamie, about to leave for the evening, has one of her flashcards.

JAMIE. What are the main causes of postoperative fever?

PENELOPE. The five Ws. Wind, water, wound, walking, and wonder drugs. Wind meaning lungs, including pneumonia, aspiration, and pulmonary embolism. Water meaning UTI, usually catheter-associated. Wound: infection in the incision. Walking meaning deep vein thrombosis, aka a blood clot, usually in the legs hence walking, but it can travel to the lungs if it goes undetected for too long, which is not uncommon. Wonder drugs meaning, fever caused by the medication used, often jokingly referred to as the "What did we do?" W.

Maybe they high-five or something fun and competitive.

You smell good. You *look* good.

JAMIE. Well, I want to make it crystal clear you married the right one.

PENELOPE. Is that so?

JAMIE. Want me to bring back anything?

PENELOPE. Mmmmmm—Nilla Wafers? Tostitos? Anything beige.

JAMIE. You got it.

PENELOPE. What are you guys seeing?

JAMIE. One guess.

PENELOPE. Uhhhh *Alvin and the Chipmunks 2: The Squeakquel.*

JAMIE. Close.

PENELOPE. Oh. *Wolverine.*

JAMIE. Bye.

Jamie starts to walk out.

PENELOPE. Kiss me goodbye.

He walks back and kisses her.

JAMIE. Have fun with the five Ws.

PENELOPE. I slept with him.

JAMIE. Dude. I know.

PENELOPE. Two weeks before our wedding.

JAMIE. "Goodbye dear."

PENELOPE. It was so dumb. I got drunk. It was—so dumb.

JAMIE. Wait, you slept with Otis two weeks before our wedding.

PENELOPE. In a bar bathroom, like a tiny little tart. It lasted five minutes. Less than that.

JAMIE. You are definitely not joking right now.

PENELOPE. No.

Pause.

JAMIE. How did that, um. Happen?

Pause.

PENELOPE. So he called me.
I was on the way home from the hospital. He suggested we grab a quick drink. I did, and—
It was not a quick drink.

JAMIE. Why are you telling me this—

PENELOPE. I / don't know.

JAMIE. —now?

Pause.

PENELOPE. I dunno. Because. I dunno. Because. I didn't even *want* to do it, I didn't. But. I did. And. I guess I'd rather you be mad at me— very mad. Very very mad. Than—have something I—can't tell you.

Pause. He doesn't react. At all.

Jamie, you know everything about me. Like, *everything*.
And you love me. And that—
That—
That is the bedrock of my life.
I think plenty of people feel loved *enough*. They have—companionship.
I don't think everyone feels known, really *known*. Not like I do, by you.
I don't want to have a secret from you.
I'd rather hurt you than have—
Something I can't tell you.

JAMIE. What do you mean you didn't want to do it?

PENELOPE. I mean, I *did* do it. I'm not saying—
I did it. I'm not saying I didn't.
I *did* do it.
But it was—
It was like—

Pause.

I was *determined* to not get drunk. I specifically said to myself, before he got there, I'm *not* going to drink because I know how he is—

JAMIE. And you know how you are.

PENELOPE. And I know how *I* am, yes. But—then, I *did* drink. He kept buying rounds or tipping the bartender so much *she'd* buy

54

more rounds. Dude, I am *not* trying to weasel out of this. Like. At *all*. I did do it. And I'm here for that meeting but.

    Pause.*

I didn't feel *set up* exactly, but.
I did feel—
Like.
Like.
Like.
Like.
Like.
I dunno. I'm sorry.
The point is I'm sorry.
I made a mistake and I'm sorry.

    Pause.

It felt bad, Jamie. Really really bad.

JAMIE. I mean, I should hope so.

    Pause.

Did he wear a condom?

PENELOPE. No.

JAMIE. Did he finish inside you?

PENELOPE. No.

JAMIE. Are you sure?

PENELOPE. Yes.

JAMIE. You were drunk enough to feel—degraded—but not so drunk you forgot where he finished.

PENELOPE. That is correct.

JAMIE. Have you—

    Pause.

PENELOPE. Done the math? Yeah. We're good.

JAMIE. Yeah?

PENELOPE. *(This is the truth.)* Yeah.

---

* In the inarticulate lines that follow this pause, a difficult but not at all understood memory of Penelope's almost rises to the surface; just before it reaches her consciousness, however, she pushes it back down and apologizes to Jamie.

Pause.

JAMIE. Okay.

PENELOPE. I'm sorry.

Pause.

Are you mad? Of course you're mad. I guess I want to—
Hear from you.

JAMIE. I dunno. Not really. I mean, sure, I guess but. I dunno. I'm not sure…
How I feel.

PENELOPE. Do you wish I hadn't said anything?

Pause.

JAMIE. I'm gonna go.

PENELOPE. To—*Wolverine*?

JAMIE. To *Wolverine the Squeakquel*.

He laughs. He can't help himself.

2009
Jamie and Otis

A bar. Jamie and Otis are drinking beers. They just saw Wolverine.

OTIS. I liked it!

JAMIE. I did too.

OTIS. Me too. I liked it a lot. I mean, it's not a "high quality film," I know but—I just love that character.

JAMIE. Same. I applied to work at his kids' school. Hugh Jackman's kids.

OTIS. What school?

JAMIE. Little Red School House? In Manhattan?

OTIS. Sure. Sure. I think David Bowie's kid goes there too.

JAMIE. No shit.

OTIS. Rebecca's job is near there. She's seen him a few times.

JAMIE. That's a solid New York Sighting.

OTIS. It is. It is. Are you still waiting to hear? About the job?

JAMIE. Oh. No. I didn't get it. That was like two years ago.

OTIS. Their loss.

JAMIE. It's cool. I quit anyway and—leapt into the unknown.

OTIS. Quit teaching?

JAMIE. For the Board of Ed, yeah. I started an education consulting service with a teacher buddy of mine about a year ago.

OTIS. Did I know that?

JAMIE. Penelope didn't tell you?

OTIS. I don't think so. But I don't think I've seen her in—man, how long has it been?

JAMIE. Well, our wedding.

OTIS. Right. Duh. Your wedding.
But yeah, it feels like we don't see you guys anymore.
Cheers.

JAMIE. Cheers.
How's ArtStart going?

OTIS. Honestly? I'm tired. I think I've got one more push in me and then that's it.
I hired a new office manager. Megan. We'll see if that turns things around. I mean, she's no Penelope, but...

Pause.

How is Penelope?

JAMIE. She just finished year one of her surgery internship.

OTIS. That is so fucking cool.

JAMIE. It's—hell.

OTIS. Oh.

JAMIE. I mean, you know her. She's a nerd, she loves—digging around through people's organs and shit, but it's the surgeons, you know. That whole like, boys' club.

OTIS. Oh.

JAMIE. There's a lot of ritual humiliation.
>   *Pause.*

OTIS. Tell her hi, will you?

JAMIE. Of course.
>   *Pause.*

And uh, she's pregnant.

OTIS. No shit! Congrats man.

JAMIE. Yeah, thanks. I can't bring myself to say "we're pregnant."

OTIS. Sure.

JAMIE. Because it's—not true.

OTIS. This is big news. I should—should I text her?

JAMIE. We're not supposed to tell people yet. It's a little too soon to celebrate.

OTIS. Got you. So I don't know?

JAMIE. I mean whatever.

OTIS. Cool. You guys move quick.

JAMIE. It happened a little sooner than we planned but.

OTIS. Well, Max was a lot later than we planned and, if you don't mind my saying, yours is the better problem.

JAMIE. Totally. Though I'm pretty sure no one *ever* thought the best time to be *with child* was during your surgery internship but.

OTIS. Fair.

JAMIE. She keeps talking about how Ruth Bader Ginsberg had a baby in law school and blazed through the courts against gender discrimination with a toddler so.

OTIS. There you go.

JAMIE. We talk about Ruth Bader Ginsberg a lot.

OTIS. You guys are going to be great parents.

JAMIE. Thanks.

OTIS. I really like being Max's dad.

JAMIE. Yeah?

OTIS. It's fun. He's such a great little person and—

Fatherhood has made me—better.

> *Pause.*

I'm a better father than man.

JAMIE. Huh.

Hey, uh.

Okay, this is awkward but hopefully it won't be.

OTIS. What's up?

JAMIE. Penelope said—she told me something—

> *They catch eyes.*

I always wanted to say something, but it's weird to bring up.

OTIS. Okay.

JAMIE. The summer after she left for Stanford, when we still weren't speaking. Except for one uhhh *relapse* when she came through town and slept over. Do you know what I'm talking about?

> *Pause.*

She didn't tell me what happened until—later but.

She said you took her. She said you paid for it.

> *Otis looks at his drink. He nods.*

I just wanted to say thanks for being there for her when I wasn't. I was—too busy being a dick.

OTIS. All good, chief. You guys were young. I was much worse at that age, I promise.

Are you going to find out if it's a boy or girl?

JAMIE. We're actually kind of fighting about that.

OTIS. You want to be surprised and she wants to find out?

JAMIE. Other way around. I want to know and Penelope wants it to be a surprise.

> *Jamie raises his beer but pauses before drinking it.*

Actually I didn't like the movie. I thought it was dumb.

> *Otis looks at Jamie in surprise.*

I don't know why I pretended to like it.

> *James takes the final sip of beer and sets the bottle down. Done.*

In the transition out of the bar, we hear Penelope's outgoing voicemail message: "Hey, it's Penelope. Sorry I missed your call. Leave a message and I'll get back to you as soon as I can."

2018
Whitney

Whitney, alone on stage, is on her cell phone.

WHITNEY. Hey, Penelope. Um. It's Whitney. Hope you're good. Sorry my voice is shaking. This has nothing to do with the um, story, by the way. Whatever you decide, I'm just glad we're back in touch.

A split second to summon courage.

I'm applying to programs to become a medical assistant? There's one in Newark with a really good payment plan. I know: *Newark*, right? Anyway. I was wondering if you'd write me a letter of recommendation? I know there's a lot on your plate 'cause of—being a surgeon, so it's cool if you can't—obviously—But. I get the feeling you—see my potential?

She winces at that cringy phrase.

I hope you're having a great day. I'm not. But I'm still—proud of us. Okay. Bye.

2018
Penelope and Otis

City Hall, Otis's office. He's working. A knock.

OTIS. Come in.

Penelope enters. He looks up, happy to see her.

Hi.

PENELOPE. Can I close the door?

OTIS. Of course.

> *He stands. In the past, a closed door is an invitation. She knows this.*

PENELOPE. I did it.
I joined the story. I named myself. And I corroborated stuff that—
You don't ever want Rebecca to know. Or Max. Or—anyone.

> *Pause.*

The story wasn't quite strong enough without me but. Me joining made it—strong enough to run. I said a lot of nice things about you. True things. But.
I told on you.

> *Pause.*

I'm sorry.

OTIS. Don't be sorry.

PENELOPE. I *am*.

OTIS. You didn't make a mistake. Don't apologize for my mistake. Mistakes.

> *A moment between them, unlike any they've ever shared. Their first as equals.*
>
> *He sits. She moves to him. She might put her hand on his back, or touch his hair. He is on the verge of an honest-to-god breakdown.*
>
> *Eventually, he looks up at her.*

Go somewhere with me?

PENELOPE. What?

OTIS. For a little while?

> *Pause.*

PENELOPE. Sure.

2018
Penelope and Otis

A short-stay motel room. Penelope and Otis are in bed. They've had sex. It was good, maybe even great, for extremely complicated reasons.

PENELOPE. God, I forgot what these places *smell* like.

They smell like cigarettes, Clorox and human desperation. Otis might chuckle in recognition but now that the sex is over, reality is harder to ignore. Penelope senses where his thoughts are.

You should ask Rebecca to make a statement of support for Max's sake.

OTIS. You have got to be kidding.

PENELOPE. She'll say no at first, but then her mind will start—thinking it over, like it or not—

OTIS. There's no way.

PENELOPE. It's a long shot, but it's a shot. But only if you bring it up.

OTIS. "Nothing to zero."

PENELOPE. Hmm?

OTIS. Nothing to zero! You don't remember that?

PENELOPE. Maybe rings a bell?

OTIS. Really? Man, I think about that all the time. You said the biggest leap—we were talking about my childhood, and where I ended up versus my brother Brian—

PENELOPE. Okay.

OTIS. You said the biggest leap is—

He takes a moment to remember it right.

The biggest leap is *not* when something goes from impossible to possible. It's not knowing a thing even exists—to—believing it's impossible.

PENELOPE. Actually I don't remember, but I like it.

OTIS. What?! The leap isn't "zero to one," it's "nothing to zero"?

> *She shrugs.*

Man. That was the truest damn thing I ever heard in my life.

> *He laughs a little. She smiles.*

Anyway. That's what you're talking about. With Rebecca making a statement. I'll ask her and she'll say it's impossible.

PENELOPE. You've got two things in your favor: She loves Max and she loves you.

OTIS. She loves Max.

PENELOPE. She loves you.

OTIS. How do you know?

PENELOPE. Because she gave you her life.
What you're up against is her humiliation. For her, that might be bigger than what you actually *did*—

OTIS. Pen. You don't have to fix this for me.

PENELOPE. *(Embarrassed.)* I know, I'm not.

OTIS. Everything that's coming I had coming. Only thing to do is—
Let it come.
Just let it come.

PENELOPE. Sure.

> *Pause.*

Is that a little—

> *Why does "let it come" irritate her so much? She searches, agitated.*

Lazy? Otis. You have to—

> *Pause.*

Give them their *meeting*! *All* of them. All of—
Us. "Let it come" sounds—absent.
The lawyer, at the *Times*—she told *Jamie* to change his cell phone number. *Jamie.* The mayor's enemies are *motivated* dude. Not to mention his—

OTIS. Allies.

PENELOPE. Allies! These guys are coming for us. And Vee and

Whitney—they put themselves out there. Whitney is scared. This is *scary*. It makes *us* feel like criminals. But we're doing it so—
Well, we're *not* doing it so you can—put your head down and wait.

OTIS. Uhhh, / okay—

PENELOPE. *Be worthy.*

OTIS. I don't know what the fuck to do, Pen. Like, what am I actually supposed to do?

Pause. She doesn't really know either.

PENELOPE. Arrange a sleepover for Max tonight so you can talk to Rebecca. You'll be up all night. She'll need space to scream and cry and…stuff like that.

Pause.

OTIS. That's a good idea.

PENELOPE. Did it feel different?

He reaches for her.

OTIS. Because my life is about to end?

PENELOPE. Because two kids crawled out since the last time you were—in there.

OTIS. Oh. No. It felt great.

PENELOPE. It didn't feel different?

OTIS. It did. It felt different and great.

Pause.

PENELOPE. I should probably, uh…

Penelope checks the time on her cell. Otis looks at her phone too.

OTIS. Whitney Bauer. You guys are buds now?

PENELOPE. Yeah, kinda.

She laughs a little. Then she stops.
Then she laughs a little harder.

OTIS. What?

She starts to laugh hysterically. Otis certainly doesn't get what she's laughing about. She might not either, as this catharsis possesses her and becomes a prolonged, full-body experience.

At last she pulls herself together.

PENELOPE. I should go.
I have to go.

2004
Penelope, Whitney, Otis, and Ken

The ArtStart office. Penelope is showing Whitney a binder but Whitney is pretty distracted by her T-Mobile Sidekick.

PENELOPE. Here, I put together this binder to help you get oriented. The first page is a flow chart of all the steps you have to do, from when Otis books a new client, all the way to the group thank-you note to the parents, which we all sign and present on the last day at the mural party.
She looks at Whitney, who's on her phone.
Can you—
Hear me, Whitney?
WHITNEY. Sorry, there's a—*auggh* what the fuck is wrong with him? Sorry. The binder. My dad is being psycho and it's really distracting. Hi.
PENELOPE. Where do you go to college, Whitney?
WHITNEY. Parsons. And I just graduated.
PENELOPE. Congratulations.
WHITNEY. Thanks.
PENELOPE. Everything's divided into four categories. Money, supplies, children, and teaching artists.
Whitney is on her Sidekick again.
You got that?
WHITNEY. Totally.
PENELOPE. What are the four categories?
Whitney has no clue.
WHITNEY. ...money?

PENELOPE. This stuff is important because we work with people's kids. Their / *children*—

WHITNEY. Augghhhh!

PENELOPE. Do you want to come back tomorrow?

WHITNEY. No. This is great.

PENELOPE. This is a complicated job.

WHITNEY. Oh, is it a—bad job?

PENELOPE. It's a *wonderful* job but there are a lot of details.

WHITNEY. I so appreciate this binder you made. That's going to help a lot, I can tell.

PENELOPE. Please put your phone away.

WHITNEY. Okay.

PENELOPE. We're counting on you to be professional. Do you think you're acting professional right / now?

WHITNEY. Can I just make a really quick phone call? Super quick.

PENELOPE. No.

WHITNEY. Okay.

PENELOPE. Why don't you sit here, read through this, and when you have a question, ask me.

WHITNEY. Cool.

> *Whitney accepts the binder—and immediately resumes texting. Back to the binder. Back to her texts.*
>
> *Penelope watches with frustration she can barely contain.*
>
> *We hear Otis and Ken before we see them.*

KEN. Thank you. I'm sorry. She's very angry at me.

OTIS. Not at all. Not at all.

> *Otis and Ken enter. Otis is carrying a detachable infant car seat. Little baby Max is sleeping inside.*

KEN. First, she just *has* to go to college in New York City. Now it's this new job—in *Brooklyn*.

WHITNEY. Oh my god Dad are you serious? Are you serious right now!

OTIS. You must be Whitney. Hi, I'm Otis. We spoke on the phone.

WHITNEY. Hi, nice to meet you, I'm so so sorry, he *always* does this, he's the literal *worst*.

OTIS. Not at all. Not at all. I bumped into Ken outside and offered to give him a tour of the office. This is Penelope, our fearless captain who is leaving us next month, for Stanford Medical School.

WHITNEY. Dad! Turn around right now.

KEN. *(To Otis, explaining himself.)* I grew up in *Detroit* so I consider myself something of a—I actually know my way around some of this—inner city stuff.

WHITNEY. "Inner city," Dad! Really?

KEN. / What.

OTIS. Wait, wait, wait.
Detroit?

KEN. Yeah.

OTIS. Good year to be from Detroit!

KEN. I—love—that—TEAM SO MUCH!

OTIS. Don't ask me how much money I lost.

KEN. How much money did you lose?

OTIS. I'll never tell. Who bets against Kobe?!

KEN. Me. Because I bet on *defense* baby, because—what wins championships? Is it offense? *(To Whitney.)* Is it offense?

WHITNEY. *(Annoyed but trained.)* No, it's defense.

KEN. Defense! *Defense* wins championships.

OTIS. Kobe broke my fuckin' heart man. *(Re: language.)* Excuse me, Whitney.

KEN. Broke it with a little help from Shaq.

OTIS. And Malone. And Gary Payton. Man.

KEN. Sorry but, when you got Ben Wallace in the paint bringing down the boards—

OTIS. And the other Wallace! Both Wallaces. Sheed!

KEN. A seven-footer draining threes. Not much you can do about that, not even Kobe.

OTIS. Not even Kobe.
Yeah, that was some beautiful basketball. And it cost me a lot of money. In five! *Five!*

KEN. Five!

OTIS. *Five!* Man. If at some point you're moved to buy me a drink, Ken…

They both laugh.

WHITNEY. See?

KEN. What?

WHITNEY. Nice office, Stanford Medical School, the Pistons, you can leave now! I'm so so sorry.

KEN. Yes. Wanting your children to grow into full adulthood is *so embarrassing*.

OTIS. No problem. No problem. I grew up in Brooklyn and where I'm from, at that time, there was—plenty to be concerned about. But I assure you, this is an extremely safe area and we are very careful on the mural sites.

KEN. I'm sure you are. It's just strange, you know? Knowing she's out in the world, a free agent. She's our only kid and—

PENELOPE. Ken. May I call you Ken?

KEN. Please.

PENELOPE. Maybe you want to take a look at this. I put together a kind of—scrap book of our last three murals. Look. These are the kids. That's Michael. That's little Cosi. She's my heart. Here's a bunch of thank-you notes they wrote the teachers and Otis. They love Otis. He's like—everyone's favorite big brother.
That's our most recent one, in Harlem. It's two stories tall! We were standing on scaffolding for that one!

KEN. Wow.

PENELOPE. I love thinking about all the people who live and work in that neighborhood. That mural is a part of their lives, their memories.

KEN. That's great.

Otis didn't know about these books.

PENELOPE. This is a wonderful place to work.

OTIS. When did you make that?

PENELOPE. It's a little—side project. I was going to surprise you on my last day, but I thought it might be put to better use now.

> *Otis is very touched. He and Penelope beam at one another while Whitney and Ken flip through the album.*

KEN. This seems like a really special place.

OTIS. I think it is.

> *The baby wakes up and makes a little noise.*

PENELOPE. Oh oh oh. Can I hold him?

2018
Penelope and Otis

> *The motel room. Penelope is waiting, fully dressed. Her coat is on. Otis comes in from his shower. In a towel, probably. He's surprised to see Penelope, dressed and waiting.*

PENELOPE. Do you remember the first time I got you hard?

OTIS. Hi, Pen.

PENELOPE. I'm really asking you this. When was the first time I got you hard?

OTIS. I don't know.

PENELOPE. Early on? Probably?

OTIS. Probably.

PENELOPE. Were you hard on my first day of work? Or, was it even earlier?
My interview? When I cried about my "dead brother," were you like…?

> *She doesn't care to finish that thought.*

Was it *before* the interview? Ha! Did you see my name and school at the top of my resume and think, oooh, Ivy League Girls Gone Wild, *what's that like?*

OTIS. Why are you—

PENELOPE. Because I want to know how it starts! When did Whitney first get you hard?

OTIS. I don't / know.

PENELOPE. Because she told *me*, that during her interview—her *phone* interview, with you—she said you said, "Are you also an actor? You have a great speaking voice." You hadn't even *laid eyes* on her yet.

Otis. Whitney does *not* have a great speaking voice. What were you *doing*?

> *Pause.*

I thought she was so unprofessional.
I looked *down* on her when I should have been looking *out* for her. Protecting her. From you!

> *Pause.*

Our interview is one of my favorite memories.

OTIS. Me too.

PENELOPE. But we're not having the same memory, right? My memories are wrong. 'Cause *I* thought—god I was dumb—I thought you and I rose across a *vast divide*. In age, work station—*marriage*—I thought we crossed these huge distances because something beautiful and rare was slowly being born just because we were near each other every day. I didn't wonder about other women! Whitney, Vee, Marissa? Rebecca?! I should have thought about Rebecca. I knew better, even then, but.
All I could think about was you.
Otis, I feel so stupid. And I don't know if I'm supposed to look at that girl who fell for you and *forgive her*, for being—a *girl*—or if I'm *still* that girl, looking through the sheets for evidence that you love me like a fucking idiot!
Who were you? Who *are* you? And if every one of us who walks through your door is first and foremost fuckable, who are we? Are we people? Like, *real people*?

> *Pause.*

What do you think, Otis?

OTIS. What do I *think*?
PENELOPE. Yes!
OTIS. I don't know!
I love you.

>   *This pisses her off, a lot actually, but she sets anger aside. She wants a meeting, not a war.*

PENELOPE. What you do looks like love, it looks *exactly like* love but—

>   *Pause.*

It positions me to serve you. I'm here to serve you, right? I'm here to serve you *me*. And—I did! I fed you. God, I loved feeding myself to you. I got dressed for work every morning and I couldn't wait.

>   *Pause.*

You know what Vee said?

>   *She laughs.*

Vee said: If they're going to give up their power, we've got to give up their power too. Isn't that—smart?

>   *Pause. He gives her nothing.*

What were mornings like for you?
What's it like riding the subway to work, knowing you'll see the top of my head? I imagine it's wonderful.

>   *Pause.*

Goddamnit, Otis, *why won't you talk to me?*

>   *Pause.*

You're not going to talk to me, right?
Right. I'm at this meeting alone.

OTIS. You didn't call a meeting, Pen. You called the *New York Times*.

>   *Pause.*

Whitney, Vee, Keilynn. They don't have me. Them in the news, I get it. I hate it, but I get it. I deserve it. But you can't get your meeting, are you kidding? Are you fucking kidding? I *always* take your call, Pen. I always text you back. I text you back in meetings, on vacation. You *have* me. You could have asked me whatever you wanted whenever you wanted but you didn't ask me *anything*. You

71

didn't call a meeting with *me*. You called a meeting with *Rebecca*. You called a meeting with the *mayor*. You called a meeting with everyone who reads the news and everyone who looks me up, from the day that story runs until I *die*. This story is all I am, forever. But we're gonna search our souls together now? Is that the plan? You brought *(He can barely say his name.)* Max—to our meeting. *Max.* I might not get to raise him.

Even if Rebecca doesn't—take him—which she absolutely might— he might—

    Pause.

Never speak to me again.

It is possible Max will never speak to me ever again, because you—

    He can't fucking believe this shit.

I don't love *you*? Really? *You told on me.* You told on me.

PENELOPE. I told on you BECAUSE I love you! I TOLD ON YOU BECAUSE I LOVE YOU OTIS!

I told on you *because* I love you.

OTIS. Of all the people in the world to—

    Pause.

I *never* thought it would be you. I'd have bet my life on that. I'd have bet my fucking life that you would never—

PENELOPE. Tell the truth? *I said what happened.* All I said is what we did.

I think we have to tell the truth. We have to try. We have to look at this, together, we have to tell the truth, together. I look at what I did to Vee. How *easily* I dismissed Whitney. I see that and it is—*not flattering* but—it's better than pretending. It's better than hiding, it really is.

I think you shouldn't be afraid. You don't have to be afraid.

OTIS. Thanks, I'll remember that.

PENELOPE. Dude. Remember how much we *lied*? We lied to everyone. All the time. You *taught* me how to lie. About where I was, who I was with, what I was doing. It was fun. Those lies felt like a secret portal to another land, and in that land you were *king*. You're a king, but. I think you have to stop lying now.

Who are we, to you? And if hiring us gets you hard, WHO ARE YOU? What if you asked yourself that? And what if, when you answered, you told the fucking truth! Doesn't that sound better? Doesn't that sound like *freedom*? I want that for you *because* I love you but I cannot do it for you.

OTIS. If I show myself to you, you won't love me.

PENELOPE. Looks like we'll never know.

> *She heads for the door. She tried. She really did.*

When I came back in here, I thought you were gonna do better. I really did.

OTIS. Wait.

Pen. Wait.

Don't give up on me.

> *She faces him. He faces her. He tries. He wants to try.*

I—
I—
I—
I—
I—
I—

> *He stops trying for a while. Then—*

I don't know where to start.

PENELOPE. Am I a person?

OTIS. What?

PENELOPE. Am I a person. The way you are a person. The way Max is a person. The way *Marvin the Martian* is a fucking / person—

OTIS. Of course.

PENELOPE. Is Vee?

> *No.*

Whitney?

> *No.*

Marissa? Keilynn? Megan?

> *No. None of them.*

No. They're not. They can't be sex *and* a person.

> *She might choke on this thought.*

And neither can I.

> *Pause.*

Am I a person?

> *Otis looks at her and asks himself this question; he comes to the meeting.*
>
> *Is Penelope a person?*
> *He doesn't know. Then he does.*
>
> *The answer is no.*
> *They both feel this.*
> *He is devastated. She might be too, but she may also be relieved. The truth is a relief.*

OTIS. I'm sorry, Pen.

PENELOPE. I'm gonna go but I want you to do something for me.

OTIS. I'm sorry.

PENELOPE. You're going to give me a gift.

OTIS. Okay.

PENELOPE. When the story comes out, read it with Max. He's going to read it anyway. Read it together. And tell him, he can ask you whatever he wants, whenever he wants. Could be today, could be in ten years, but you will *always* give Max his meeting about this. And at that meeting, you will tell the truth. Promise me.

OTIS. I can't show myself to Max. That would be—
Impossible.

> *They look at each other. Penelope smiles; he just made the biggest leap.*

2018
Jamie and Penelope

Jamie and Penelope's bedroom. It's the middle of the night. Jamie is awake, reading on a laptop. He nudges Penelope.

JAMIE. You ready? It posted.

She sits up, carefully, preparing herself. They look at each other. She nods. He hands her the laptop. She reads.

PENELOPE. Wow. I *really* thought I was special, didn't I.

JAMIE. You were there. If you thought you were special, you were.

PENELOPE. I thought I was the only one.

JAMIE. Except Vee.

Pause.

You knew about Vee.

PENELOPE. No, I didn't.

JAMIE. You're the one who told *me*.

PENELOPE. I did?

JAMIE. Yes. That was a hundred percent why I—

PENELOPE. Really?

JAMIE. Yes.

PENELOPE. *Really?*

JAMIE. Yes.

Pause.

How did it feel to—uh…

JAMIE. What?

PENELOPE. Um, to, I guess, have sex with Vee and never talk to her again?

Pause.

JAMIE. *(No trace of pride, just honesty.)* Felt pretty good.

Pause.

PENELOPE. It felt good to me too.

Shit.
I should call her.
See if she wants to—get tea.

They keep reading the article.

JAMIE. This part makes it sound pretty hot.

PENELOPE. It was.

JAMIE. I know, I'm just surprised they—leaned into that angle.

They keep reading together. Penelope reacts to something, and points to the screen.

I know. That whole paragraph sounds like my mom.

PENELOPE. It really does, oh my god.

She abruptly closes the screen.

I don't know if I can finish this.

JAMIE. Of course you can.

They look at each other. Penelope keeps reading.

PENELOPE. Jamie. I'm—this feels like I'm— *(Laughs.)* dying. Something is dying. I thought I was ready to let it die but—

JAMIE. Penelope.

Pause.

Pen.

PENELOPE. What.

JAMIE. Let it die.
You don't—

PENELOPE. —need it anymore.

2003
Penelope and Otis

The ArtStart office. Penelope and Otis sit facing each other. Otis is looking at a letter.

OTIS. This letter is—wow. You've seen it, right?

PENELOPE. No, actually. I've / never—

OTIS. No? For real?

She shakes her head.

Do you want to? If someone wrote this about me, I'd want to read it.

Penelope laughs politely.

Here.

Penelope actually does want to see the letter, quite badly, but she won't let herself.

PENELOPE. I think that would undermine the, um—what's the word.

Pause.

OTIS. Secret?

PENELOPE. Integrity?

OTIS. Oh, right.

PENELOPE. I mean, I don't know but.

OTIS. You're right. The whole point of the sealed envelope is…

PENELOPE. It like, authenticates the message I guess?

He looks the letter over, then looks at Penelope.

OTIS. Man. It's just—
You at this age, versus me at your age, but *I'm* hiring *you*. Okay.

PENELOPE. Hopefully.

OTIS. Oh, come on.

PENELOPE. Excuse me?

OTIS. You know you got the job.

PENELOPE. I hope I haven't seemed—presumptuous—or—

OTIS. Oh, no.

PENELOPE. I have no idea who you're hiring.

OTIS. Sure, you're right. I'm having fun while you're—
It just seems to me like—

He holds up her resume.

You've never been turned down in your life.

PENELOPE. I have definitely been turned down in my life.

OTIS. By a job?

PENELOPE. No, not by a job.

OTIS. That's all I'm saying.

PENELOPE. But I don't think I would *get* jobs if I walked into the interview assuming I'm hired.

OTIS. Huh. The advice I always got was to act like you got the job.

Penelope smiles and waits for the interview to continue.

I'm impressed that you—
This letter is dated more than a year back.
So you asked for a recommendation letter before you even knew what job you're applying for?

PENELOPE. Yes.

OTIS. That is organized! They don't teach that stuff.

PENELOPE. They do.
We were coached. That's actually exactly what they teach.

OTIS. Not at my school but I guess it makes sense that *Yale* would use that playbook. Your hobby is calligraphy?

PENELOPE. I know it's not an art like murals and stuff but.

OTIS. Cool.

PENELOPE. I'm pretty passionate about it.

Pause.

Where did you go to school?

OTIS. Michigan State.

PENELOPE. That's a great school!

OTIS. *(Teasing her.)* Thanks. Yeah.

PENELOPE. Sorry, was that…? I hope I wasn't being, like…

OTIS. I chose it because my favorite football player went there. And I got a scholarship so that was—but—I wish someone had kicked my ass a little more.
But we're not here to talk about me.

PENELOPE. No, please, I'm interested.

OTIS. Where I came from, I was a big fish in a very small pond. Everything I did was "the best." I was the best. At school. At drawing. At sports.

Pause.

But I was the best in our *yard*. In our *building*. I wish someone had told me that's not the same as being the best.

PENELOPE. Wow. Yeah.

His Palm Treo cell rings. He checks it, silences it, puts it away.

OTIS. Sorry.

PENELOPE. Feel free to take it.

OTIS. I do feel free. Thank you.

PENELOPE. Sorry, I didn't mean—

OTIS. I'm kidding.

PENELOPE. I keep insulting you by accident.

OTIS. Not at all. Where were we?

PENELOPE. You wish someone pushed you to make better choices.

He holds up her letter.

OTIS. It sounds like you've been through a lot and handled it with real…

Grace.

PENELOPE. Oh.

OTIS. I admire that.

PENELOPE. Thank you.

He gets a text, checks it, puts the phone away again.

OTIS. You're deferring medical school for a year?

PENELOPE. Yes.

OTIS. Why?

PENELOPE. I knew you were going to ask that.

She laughs nervously.

I feel like I'm at dinner with my dad.

OTIS. Don't say that. I'll hire you either way. I'm going to hire you. Now we're just talking.

PENELOPE. You're going to hire me?

OTIS. Yes.

PENELOPE. Really?

OTIS. Yes.

PENELOPE. Oh my gosh! Thank you!

OTIS. You're welcome.

PENELOPE. I can relax now. Yay. So um, yeah. I'm deferring because…
Once you're on that path, medical school, you're on it for many, many, many years. I want to be a surgeon, so.

OTIS. Wow. Okay.

PENELOPE. It's all-consuming forever and ever, basically. So. I guess I wanted to…

> *She finds herself choking up but stays on top of it. Losing her composure in an interview is unacceptable.*

Not be on a path? For like, a second?

OTIS. How old are you?

PENELOPE. Twenty-two.

OTIS. I was never on a path. Never.

PENELOPE. Not even in school?

OTIS. The truth is? I thought I was a genius. And geniuses can do whatever the fuck they want. And that's what I did. It's embarrassing.

PENELOPE. What was your—the medium of your—genius?

OTIS. Football and art.
Comics, Graffiti. *(Gesturing to the office.)* Murals, kinda.

PENELOPE. Right. ArtStart. Duh.

OTIS. I thought I was Basquiat trapped in a comic strip.
My muse was Marvin the Martian.

> *They laugh.*

Don't laugh. That's my dude.
I had to get old to realize how much stability—and a *career*—matter. To hot women.

> *He laughs. She does, too.*

Kidding. Kind of? No. I founded this organization as a way to…
This is my path. My straight and narrow.

PENELOPE. And it's working!

OTIS. My wife is a lot happier.

PENELOPE. It's actually kind of sweet how this *(Meaning this room, this job.)* is you being on track and me getting off the track.

OTIS. Yeah.

PENELOPE. That's actually kind of—

OTIS. Great.

>*Pause.*

I'm so sorry about your brother.

>*Pause.*

>*Vanessa enters.*

VANESSA. Otes?

OTIS. Vanessa, this is Penelope. She's applying to be—the other you. Penelope, Vanessa.

VANESSA. Or just Vee. Nice shoes.

PENELOPE. Thank you.

OTIS. Vanessa is our office manager and head teaching artist. She takes care of staffing our programs. Marissa used to do in-house admin.

VANESSA. Now I'm doing both, so I'm really hoping he hires you stat.

>*Penelope laughs.*

Rebecca's on line one. She sounds mad.

OTIS. Excuse me.

>*He leaves. Just Vanessa and Penelope in here.*

PENELOPE. Is everything okay?

VANESSA. It's fine. She's always mad. If he hires you, we should all get a drink to celebrate.

PENELOPE. That's so sweet, you don't have to!

VANESSA. Do you not drink or something?

PENELOPE. Oh, no. I do.

VANESSA. I was gonna say, we drink a lot here, so if you're a, whatever…

PENELOPE. I'd love to. Thank you.

VANESSA. We're kinda like a family. You're going to love it here. The kids are so fucking cute.

PENELOPE. Awesome.

Otis is back.

OTIS. I think I have to deal with some stuff. Sorry to—cut us off. What do you say, wanna come work at ArtStart with us?

PENELOPE. Oh my gosh, yes! That's amazing!

OTIS. Vee will show you out. Come back tomorrow at nine and we'll jump right in.

PENELOPE. Okay. Great! Wow.

OTIS. Sorry, we got cut off.

PENELOPE. No that's okay. See you tomorrow.

OTIS. Looking forward, Penelope.

VANESSA. I'll show you out.

OTIS. Thanks, Vee.

Once he's alone, Otis's polite face falls; he looks stressed.

He sits. He texts someone on his Palm Treo.

Penelope returns and waits in the doorway. He doesn't notice her for a long moment.

Hi.

PENELOPE. Sorry.

OTIS. How long have you been standing there?

PENELOPE. Just a second.

OTIS. What can I do for you, Penelope?

A long pause. She just stands there.

Are you okay?

PENELOPE. Yeah.
Yeah.

OTIS. Are you sure?

PENELOPE. Yeah.

But I'm about to tell you something and then, I think you won't want to hire me. But. I gotta um…
Sorry, I sort of made this promise to myself and I'm working up the nerve to keep it. Sorry, I know you don't have a lot of time.

OTIS. Sit down. I have all the time in the world.

She sits in silence for a long time.

You want some water?

PENELOPE. No thanks. You're being so nice.

OTIS. What's up?

He touches her in some way.

Penelope, what's going on?

PENELOPE. Sophomore year. Um.
I've never said this aloud before, sorry. Sophomore year, I was really stressed about finals. I was staying up late. All night. Night after night.
Um.
The guy who wrote me that letter you—have. He taught Contemporary Islamic—Civilization and he was kind of famously a jerk? But like in that cool way that makes everyone obsessed, you know? Anyway.
I had the wrong date. I was tired and I just, messed up. I thought the exam was the *next* Monday. So.
On Monday morning, the morning of the test, I'd been up all night, working on something else, I didn't even open my books for…
And I wasn't doing super well in his class in the first place. I wasn't doing super well, like, mental health–wise.
So I went to his office. And I lied.
I told a really bad lie.
I said my brother died.
And. Could I take the test on a later date.
He said sure.
And I did.
And then we—um, we actually became sorta close? He took an interest in me, academically, which was a big deal, he's a pretty famous professor. And I kept talking to him about this dead

83

brother that didn't exist. I had to update him on how my *mother* was doing…

Long pause.

If medical schools catch you lying they rescind your admission. I've seen it happen. This one girl at Yale got her admission rescinded and she jumped out her dorm window.
So, yeah. Anyway. This—you—were the first time I used his recommendation letter. This seemed like a safe place to—
Try it out. Because you are not a—
Medical school.

Pause.

Managing this lie has been so stressful, it's kind of all I think about. So, here I am. You offered me this great job, you're so great. And Vanessa said you guys are like family, she invited me to get a drink after my first day, which is so nice. I want this job, I want it a lot but.
I can't have this fake dead brother in here. I can't bring that to this office. As soon as I walked out, I knew I had to walk back in and tell you. And now you'll fire me before I even start. I'm super bummed about that. And I'm just really really sorry.

OTIS. You still have a job here, Penelope.

PENELOPE. I do?

OTIS. Definitely. Definitely. What you just did, that took real guts.

PENELOPE. Oh my god. Um. Thanks. Thank you for hiring me.

End of Play

PROPERTY LIST
(Use this space to create props lists for your production)

SOUND EFFECTS
(Use this space to create sound effects lists for your production)

Dear reader,

Thank you for supporting playwrights by purchasing this acting edition! You may not know that Dramatists Play Service was founded, in 1936, by the Dramatists Guild and a number of prominent play agents to protect the rights and interests of playwrights. To this day, we are still a small company committed to our partnership with the Guild, and by proxy all playwrights, established and aspiring, working in the English language.

Because of our status as a small, independent publisher, we respectfully reiterate that this text may not be distributed or copied in any way, or uploaded to any file-sharing sites, including ones you might think are private. Photocopying or electronically distributing books means both DPS and the playwright are not paid for the work, and that ultimately hurts playwrights everywhere, as our profits are shared with the Guild.

We also hope you want to perform this play! Plays are wonderful to read, but even better when seen. If you are interested in performing or producing the play, please be aware that performance rights must be obtained through Dramatists Play Service. This is true for *any* public performance, even if no one is getting paid or admission is not being charged. Again, playwrights often make their sole living from performance royalties, so performing plays without paying the royalty is ultimately a loss for a real writer.

This acting edition is the **only approved text for performance**. There may be other editions of the play available for sale from other publishers, but DPS has worked closely with the playwright to ensure this published text reflects their desired text of all future productions. If you have purchased a revised edition (sometimes referred to as other types of editions, like "Broadway Edition," or "[Year] Edition"), that is the only edition you may use for performance, unless explicitly stated in writing by Dramatists Play Service.

Finally, this script cannot be changed without written permission from Dramatists Play Service. If a production intends to change the script in any way—including casting against the writer's intentions for characters, removing or changing "bad" words, or making other cuts however small—without permission, they are breaking the law. And, perhaps more importantly, changing an artist's work. Please don't do that!

We are thrilled that this play has made it into your hands. We hope you love it as much as we do, and thank you for helping us keep the American theater alive and vital.

Note on Songs/Recordings, Images, or Other Production Design Elements

Be advised that Dramatists Play Service, Inc., neither holds the rights to nor grants permission to use any songs, recordings, images, or other design elements mentioned in the play. It is the responsibility of the producing theater/organization to obtain permission of the copyright owner(s) for any such use. Additional royalty fees may apply for the right to use copyrighted materials.

For any songs/recordings, images, or other design elements mentioned in the play, works in the public domain may be substituted. It is the producing theater/organization's responsibility to ensure the substituted work is indeed in the public domain. Dramatists Play Service, Inc., cannot advise as to whether or not a song/arrangement/recording, image, or other design element is in the public domain.